WELCOME TO THE U.S.A.

MONTANA

Written by Ann Heinrichs Illustrated by Matt Kania
Content Adviser: Patricia C. Spencer, Outreach and Volunteer
Coordinator, Lewis and Clark Library, Helena, Montana

The Child's World

917.86
Heinrichs

Published in the United States of America by The Child's World®
PO Box 326 • Chanhassen, MN 55317-0326
800-599-READ • www.childsworld.com

Photo Credits

Cover: Getty Images/Taxi/Scott Markewitz; frontispiece: Digital Vision.

Interior: Bannack State Park: 17; Anne Boothe/Malta Chamber of Commerce: 10; Corbis: 6 (Layne Kennedy), 14 (Macduff Everton), 18 (David Stoecklein), 21 (Brian A. Vikander), 22 (Dave G. Houser), 26 (Joel W. Rogers), 29 (D. Robert & Lorri Franz), 33 (Dale C. Sparta), 34 (Michael S. Yamashita); G. Davidson/ Red Lodge Festival of Nations: 25; Lowell Georgia/Corbis: 9, 13; Gibson & Company: 30.

Acknowledgments

The Child's World®: Mary Berendes, Publishing Director

Editorial Directions, Inc.: E. Russell Primm, Editorial Director; Katie Marsico, Associate Editor; Judith Shiffer, Assistant Editor; Matt Messbarger, Editorial Assistant; Susan Hindman, Copy Editor; Melissa McDaniel, Proofreader; Kevin Cunningham, Peter Garnham, Matt Messbarger, Olivia Nellums, Chris Simms, Molly Symmonds, Katherine Trickle, Carl Stephen Wender, Fact Checkers; Tim Griffin/IndexServ, Indexer; Cian Loughlin O'Day, Photo Researcher and Editor

The Design Lab: Kathleen Petelinsek, Design; Julia Goozen, Art Production

Library of Congress Cataloging-in-Publication Data
Heinrichs, Ann.
  Montana / by Ann Heinrichs ; cartography and illustrations by Matt Kania.
    p. cm. — (Welcome to the U.S.A.)
  Includes index.
  ISBN 1-59296-475-3 (library bound : alk. paper)
  1. Montana—Juvenile literature. I. Kania, Matt. II. Title.
  F731.3.H46 2005
  978.6—dc22   2005013219

Ann Heinrichs is the author of more than 100 books for children and young adults. She has also enjoyed successful careers as a children's book editor and an advertising copywriter. Ann grew up in Fort Smith, Arkansas, and lives in Chicago, Illinois.

**About the Author
Ann Heinrichs**

Matt Kania loves maps and, as a kid, dreamed of making them. In school he studied geography and cartography, and today he makes maps for a living. Matt's favorite thing about drawing maps is learning about the places they represent. Many of the maps he has created can be found in books, magazines, videos, Web sites, and public places.

**About the
Map Illustrator
Matt Kania**

On the cover: Yeehaw! Take a ride with a real Montana cowboy.
On page one: Look ahead! You'll see why Montana's called Big Sky Country.

OUR MONTANA TRIP

4

Are you ready to explore Montana? You'll have the adventure of a lifetime there!

You'll see gunfights and fierce battles. You'll watch exciting Native American dances. You'll round up cattle across the range. You'll see cowboys chasing madly after wild horses. You'll hang out with **wilderness** explorers. You'll climb mountains and meet wild animals. And you'll dig for dinosaur bones!

That's just a taste of what's to come. So let's head on out. Just saddle up or buckle yourself in. We're off to see Montana!

WELCOME TO MONTANA

As you travel through Montana, watch for all the interesting facts along the way.

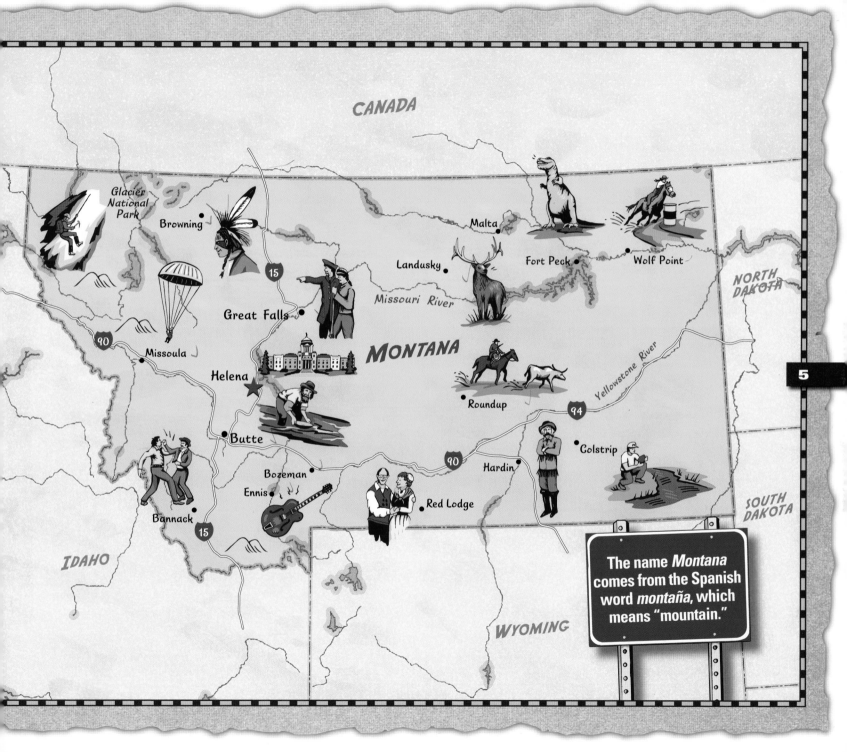

CANADA

Glacier National Park

Browning

Great Falls

Missoula

Helena

Butte

Bannack

Bozeman

Ennis

Malta

Landusky

Missouri River

MONTANA

Roundup

Fort Peck

Wolf Point

NORTH DAKOTA

Yellowstone River

Hardin

Colstrip

Red Lodge

IDAHO

WYOMING

SOUTH DAKOTA

The name *Montana* comes from the Spanish word *montaña*, which means "mountain."

Ready to explore Glacier National Park? Grab your hiking boots and hit the trails!

The Missouri River runs across northern Montana. Early explorers followed this river into the wilderness.

Glacier National Park

Do you like rugged adventures? Then you'll love Glacier National Park. It's a challenge for mountain climbers. Some mountains there have never been climbed!

Dozens of glaciers cling to the mountainsides. Glaciers are masses of snow and ice. They move along like rivers, only very slowly.

This park covers a section of the Rocky Mountains. The Rockies rise in western Montana. Their snowcapped peaks glisten in the sunlight. Many rivers cut wide valleys through the mountains. Rolling plains cover eastern Montana. Here the sky looks really big. That's why Montana is called Big Sky Country!

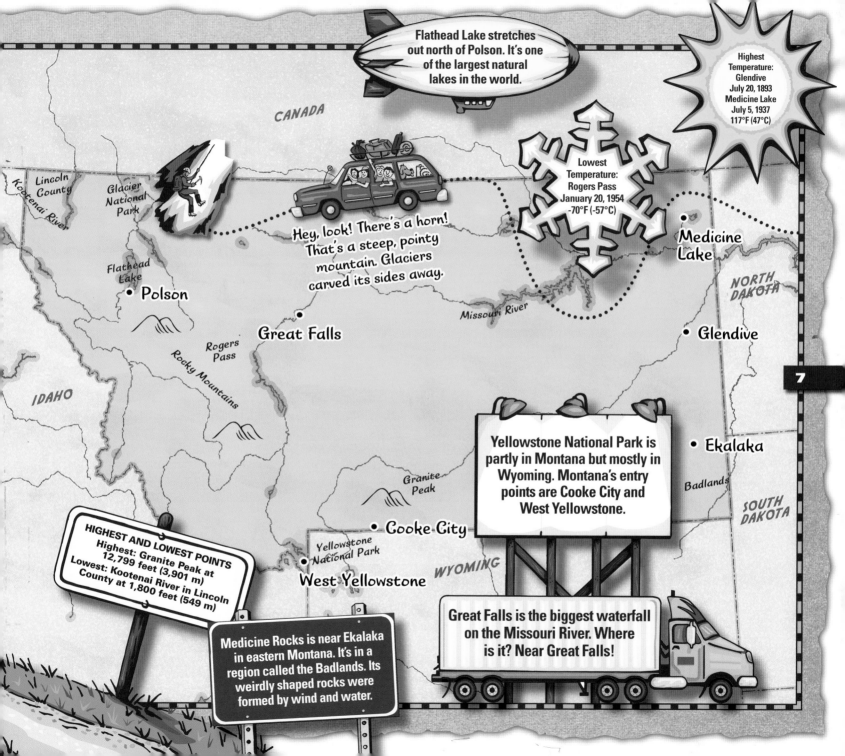

Flathead Lake stretches out north of Polson. It's one of the largest natural lakes in the world.

CANADA

Highest Temperature: Glendive July 20, 1893 Medicine Lake July 5, 1937 117°F (47°C)

Lowest Temperature: Rogers Pass January 20, 1954 -70°F (-57°C)

Lincoln County

Kootenai River

Glacier National Park

Hey, look! There's a horn! That's a steep, pointy mountain. Glaciers carved its sides away.

Flathead Lake

• Polson

Great Falls

Rogers Pass

Rocky Mountains

IDAHO

Missouri River

Medicine Lake

NORTH DAKOTA

• Glendive

• Ekalaka

Badlands

SOUTH DAKOTA

Granite Peak

HIGHEST AND LOWEST POINTS
Highest: Granite Peak at 12,799 feet (3,901 m)
Lowest: Kootenai River in Lincoln County at 1,800 feet (549 m)

• Cooke City

Yellowstone National Park

West Yellowstone

WYOMING

Yellowstone National Park is partly in Montana but mostly in Wyoming. Montana's entry points are Cooke City and West Yellowstone.

Medicine Rocks is near Ekalaka in eastern Montana. It's in a region called the Badlands. Its weirdly shaped rocks were formed by wind and water.

Great Falls is the biggest waterfall on the Missouri River. Where is it? Near Great Falls!

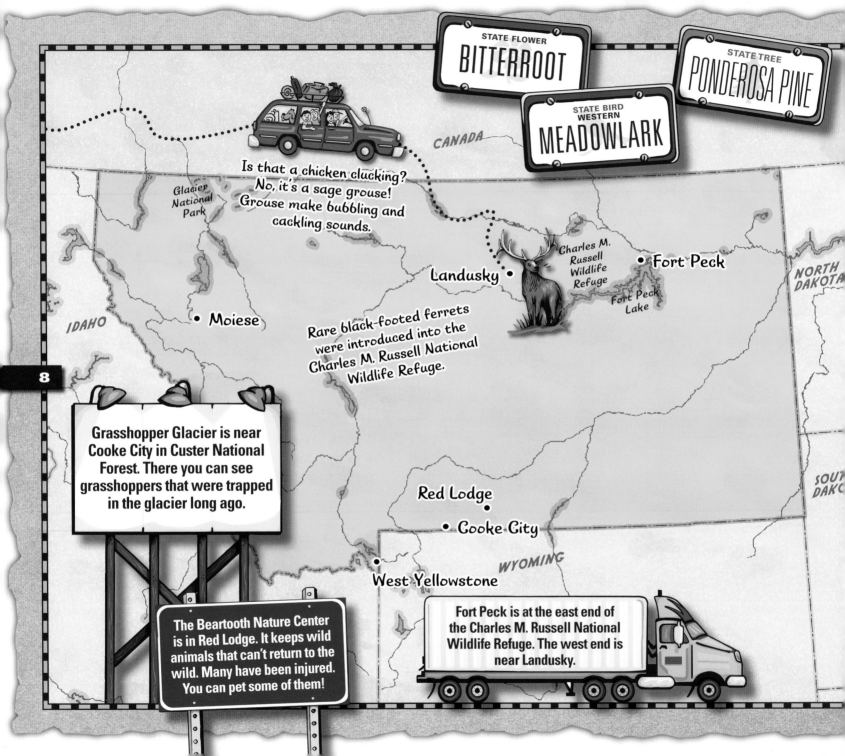

STATE FLOWER
BITTERROOT

STATE BIRD
WESTERN
MEADOWLARK

STATE TREE
PONDEROSA PINE

CANADA

Glacier National Park

Is that a chicken clucking? No, it's a sage grouse! Grouse make bubbling and cackling sounds.

Landusky

Charles M. Russell Wildlife Refuge

Fort Peck

Fort Peck Lake

NORTH DAKOTA

IDAHO

Moiese

Rare black-footed ferrets were introduced into the Charles M. Russell National Wildlife Refuge.

Grasshopper Glacier is near Cooke City in Custer National Forest. There you can see grasshoppers that were trapped in the glacier long ago.

Red Lodge

SOUTH DAKOTA

Cooke City

WYOMING

West Yellowstone

The Beartooth Nature Center is in Red Lodge. It keeps wild animals that can't return to the wild. Many have been injured. You can pet some of them!

Fort Peck is at the east end of the Charles M. Russell National Wildlife Refuge. The west end is near Landusky.

The Charles M. Russell Wildlife Refuge

The National Bison Range is near Moiese. It has herds of bison, or buffalo. Elk, deer, and antelope live there, too.

Huge elk bellow their calls. Big, woolly mountain goats look down from above. Coyotes and foxes slink through the brush. And pelicans waddle around the lakeshore.

You're exploring the Charles M. Russell National Wildlife Refuge. It runs alongside Fort Peck Lake. Do you like big animals, or tiny ones? You'll find them all here!

Glacier National Park is another great wildlife site. It has black bears, grizzly bears, and moose. Bighorn sheep paw at mountainside mosses. And graceful eagles sail through the Big Sky!

Want to do some elk-watching? Head to the Charles M. Russell Wildlife Refuge!

The National Park Service has 8 sites in Montana.

Want to see grizzly bears and gray wolves up close? Visit the Grizzly and Wolf Discovery Center near West Yellowstone.

9

Want to find a dinosaur fossil? Make your way to the Montana Dinosaur Festival!

Follow the Montana Dinosaur Trail! You'll visit 13 dinosaur museums and dig sites.

Malta's Dinosaur Festival

Would you like onions on your bronto burger? Don't worry. It's not really made of *Brontosaurus* meat. But it's a perfect snack for today's event. You're at the Montana Dinosaur Festival!

This festival celebrates some old Montana residents—dinosaurs! You'll dig for bones in a dino pit. You'll learn to make **fossil** molds. And you'll chat with the scientists who dig for dinosaurs.

Montana's a great state for dinosaur digging. Many kinds of dinosaurs once roamed here. One was *Triceratops*, with three pointy horns. Another was the fearsome *Tyrannosaurus rex*. Good thing it's not around anymore. It could have swallowed a human whole!

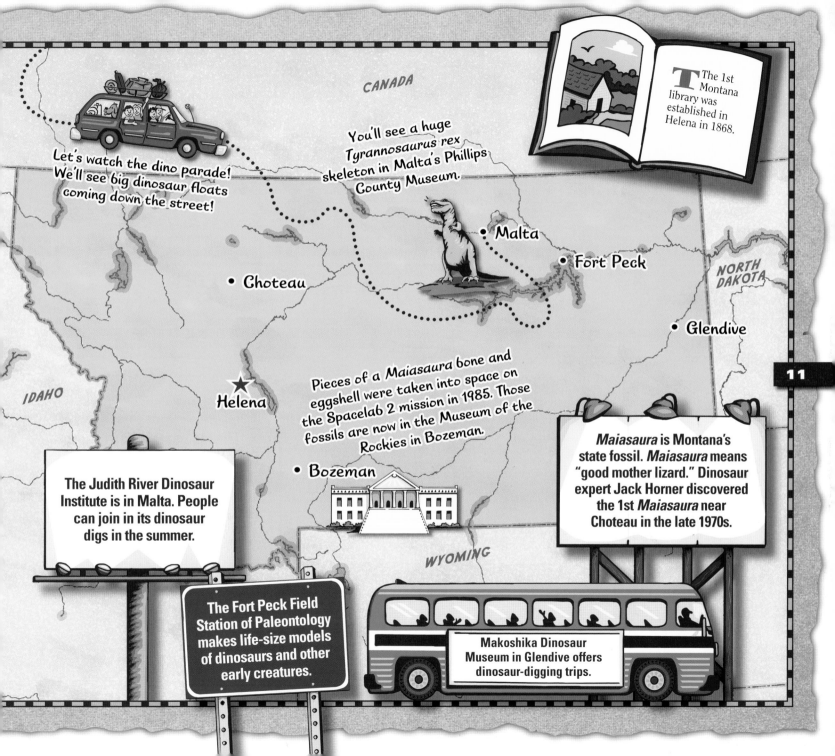

CANADA

Let's watch the dino parade! We'll see big dinosaur floats coming down the street!

You'll see a huge *Tyrannosaurus rex* skeleton in Malta's Phillips County Museum.

The 1st Montana library was established in Helena in 1868.

• Malta

• Fort Peck

NORTH DAKOTA

• Choteau

• Glendive

IDAHO

★ Helena

Pieces of a *Maiasaura* bone and eggshell were taken into space on the Spacelab 2 mission in 1985. Those fossils are now in the Museum of the Rockies in Bozeman.

Maiasaura is Montana's state fossil. *Maiasaura* means "good mother lizard." Dinosaur expert Jack Horner discovered the 1st *Maiasaura* near Choteau in the late 1970s.

• Bozeman

The Judith River Dinosaur Institute is in Malta. People can join in its dinosaur digs in the summer.

WYOMING

The Fort Peck Field Station of Paleontology makes life-size models of dinosaurs and other early creatures.

Makoshika Dinosaur Museum in Glendive offers dinosaur-digging trips.

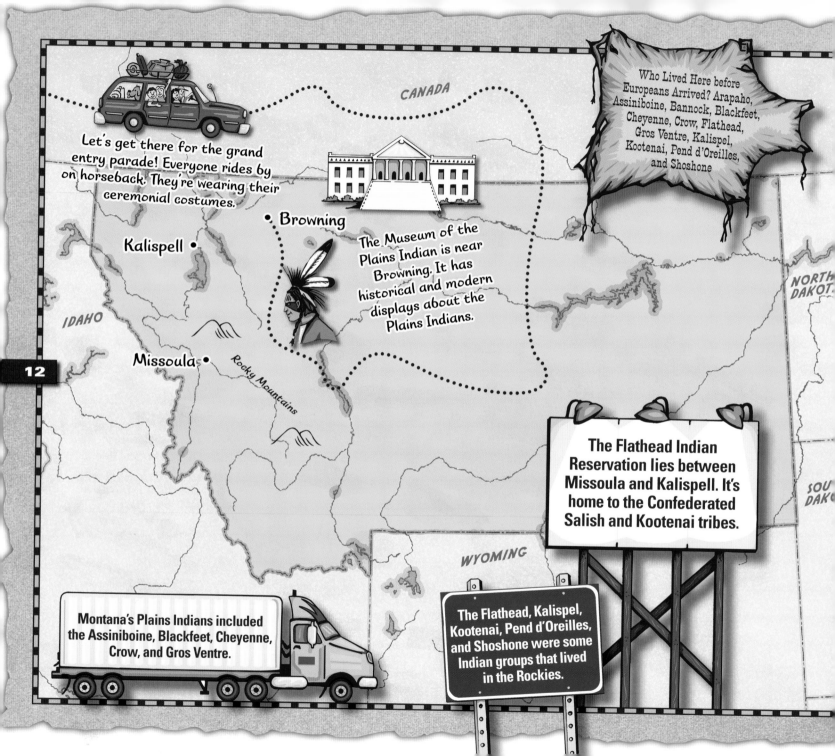

Let's get there for the grand entry parade! Everyone rides by on horseback. They're wearing their ceremonial costumes.

CANADA

Who Lived Here before Europeans Arrived? Arapaho, Assiniboine, Bannock, Blackfeet, Cheyenne, Crow, Flathead, Gros Ventre, Kalispel, Kootenai, Pend d'Oreilles, and Shoshone

Browning

Kalispell

The Museum of the Plains Indian is near Browning. It has historical and modern displays about the Plains Indians.

NORTH DAKOTA

IDAHO

Missoula

Rocky Mountains

The Flathead Indian Reservation lies between Missoula and Kalispell. It's home to the Confederated Salish and Kootenai tribes.

SOUTH DAKO

WYOMING

Montana's Plains Indians included the Assiniboine, Blackfeet, Cheyenne, Crow, and Gros Ventre.

The Flathead, Kalispel, Kootenai, Pend d'Oreilles, and Shoshone were some Indian groups that lived in the Rockies.

North American Indian Days

Want to know more about Native American culture? Head to North American Indian days!

Children and grown-ups perform ceremonial dances. Native Americans stride by on painted horses. Tall white tepees surround the camp. This is North American Indian Days! It's in Browning, on the Blackfeet Indian **Reservation.**

Indians from around the country attend this festival. Montana's Blackfeet Indians are the **hosts.** The Blackfeet are among Montana's Plains Indians. They once hunted buffalo across the eastern plains. They made clothes and tepees from buffalo hides.

Other groups made their homes in the Rockies. They gathered plants in the forests. They hunted and caught fish. They made tools from wood, bones, and rocks.

The Blackfeet are Montana's largest Indian group.

Curious about Montana's early fur traders?
Stop by the Lewis and Clark Festival!

Libby holds the Two Rivers Rendezvous every year. It recalls the fur-trade era.

The Lewis and Clark Festival in Great Falls

Mmm—smell those campfires. And what's cooking? Some nice, juicy *boudin blanc*! That's a type of sausage. Chat with the ragtag explorers around the camp. They'll show you how explorers worked and stayed alive. It's the Lewis and Clark Festival!

Explorers Meriwether Lewis and William Clark crossed Montana. They were trying to reach the Pacific Ocean. They passed through in 1805 and 1806. Their wilderness journey was tiring and dangerous.

After that, fur trappers and traders arrived. Many of the trappers were Frenchmen from Canada. One fur company built Fort Benton in 1847. That's now Montana's oldest town.

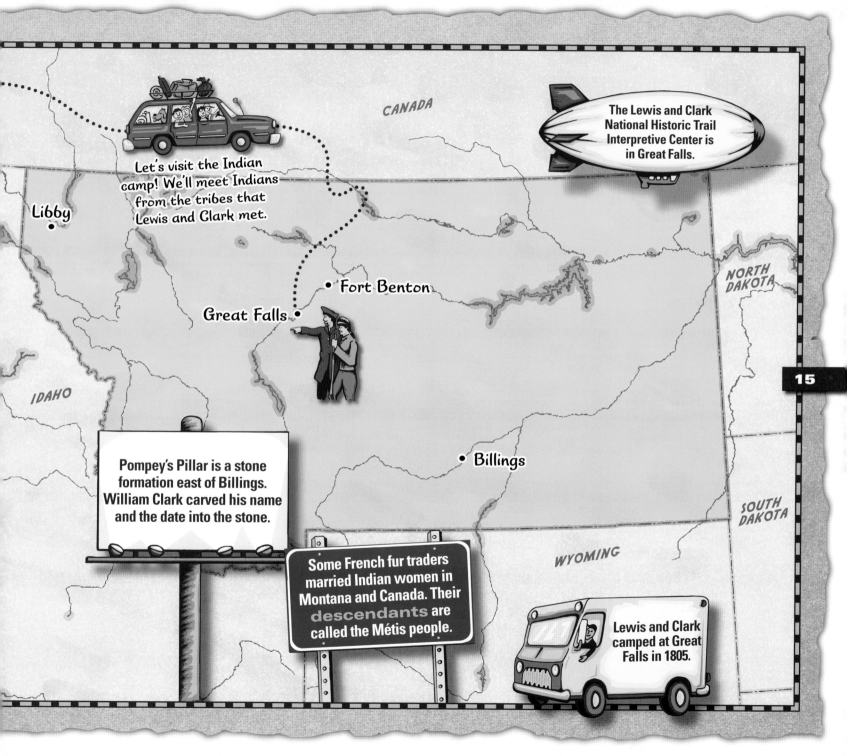

Let's visit the Indian camp! We'll meet Indians from the tribes that Lewis and Clark met.

Libby

CANADA

The Lewis and Clark National Historic Trail Interpretive Center is in Great Falls.

NORTH DAKOTA

Fort Benton

Great Falls

IDAHO

Pompey's Pillar is a stone formation east of Billings. William Clark carved his name and the date into the stone.

Billings

SOUTH DAKOTA

WYOMING

Some French fur traders married Indian women in Montana and Canada. Their descendants are called the Métis people.

Lewis and Clark camped at Great Falls in 1805.

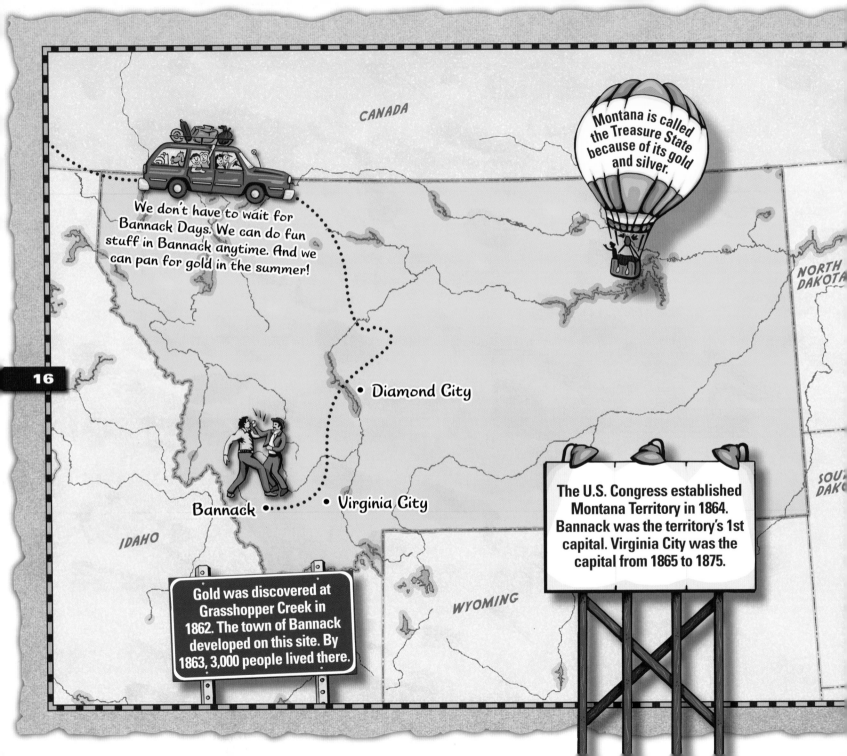

CANADA

We don't have to wait for Bannack Days. We can do fun stuff in Bannack anytime. And we can pan for gold in the summer!

Montana is called the Treasure State because of its gold and silver.

NORTH DAKOTA

• Diamond City

Bannack •

• Virginia City

IDAHO

SOUTH DAKOTA

The U.S. Congress established Montana Territory in 1864. Bannack was the territory's 1st capital. Virginia City was the capital from 1865 to 1875.

Gold was discovered at Grasshopper Creek in 1862. The town of Bannack developed on this site. By 1863, 3,000 people lived there.

WYOMING

Wild Times in Bannack

Watch a gunfight on Main Street. Ride a stagecoach through town. Chat with miners in their tent camp. It's time for Bannack Days! This event celebrates Bannack's colorful past.

Gold was discovered in Montana in 1862. Wild mining towns sprang up overnight. They included Bannack, Diamond City, and Virginia City. Outlaws roamed through the mining camps. Citizens banded together in **vigilante** groups. They hunted down outlaws and hanged them.

Meanwhile, ranchers began raising cattle in Montana. Railroads reached Montana in 1883. Then ranchers could ship cattle to faraway markets.

Could you have survived life in a mining town? Find out at Bannack Days!

Gold was found in Virginia City in 1863. It was one of the country's richest gold finds. Within a year, the town had 10,000 people.

Rounding Up Cattle in Roundup

Round 'em up, cowboy! It's time to live the cowboy life in Roundup!

Gallop across the range chasing cattle. Stop by the chuckwagon for a hearty meal. Sleep under the stars as a coyote howls. You're on the Roundup Cattle Drive!

Roundup is an old cowboy town. Cowboys are still busy in Montana. They work with cattle on Montana's many ranches. You can live the cowboy life, too. Just join the Roundup Cattle Drive!

Farms and ranches cover more than half of Montana. Beef cattle are the top farm product. Huge ranches stretch out across the plains. Some ranchers raise dairy cattle and sheep. Many farmers grow crops. Montana's top crop is wheat.

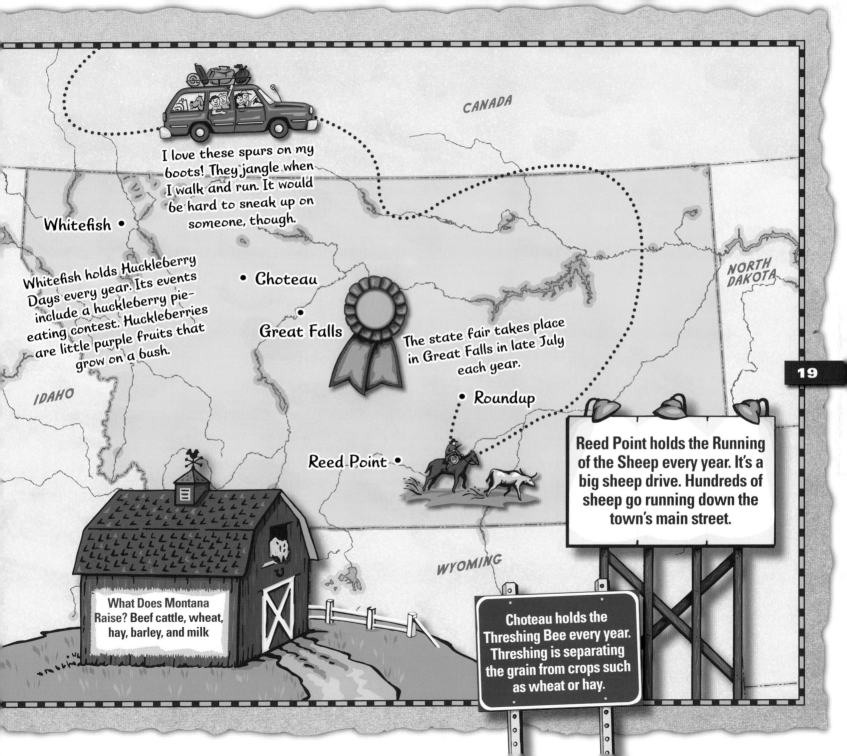

I love these spurs on my boots! They jangle when I walk and run. It would be hard to sneak up on someone, though.

CANADA

Whitefish •

Whitefish holds Huckleberry Days every year. Its events include a huckleberry pie-eating contest. Huckleberries are little purple fruits that grow on a bush.

• Choteau

• Great Falls

The state fair takes place in Great Falls in late July each year.

• Roundup

Reed Point •

NORTH DAKOTA

IDAHO

WYOMING

Reed Point holds the Running of the Sheep every year. It's a big sheep drive. Hundreds of sheep go running down the town's main street.

What Does Montana Raise? Beef cattle, wheat, hay, barley, and milk

Choteau holds the Threshing Bee every year. Threshing is separating the grain from crops such as wheat or hay.

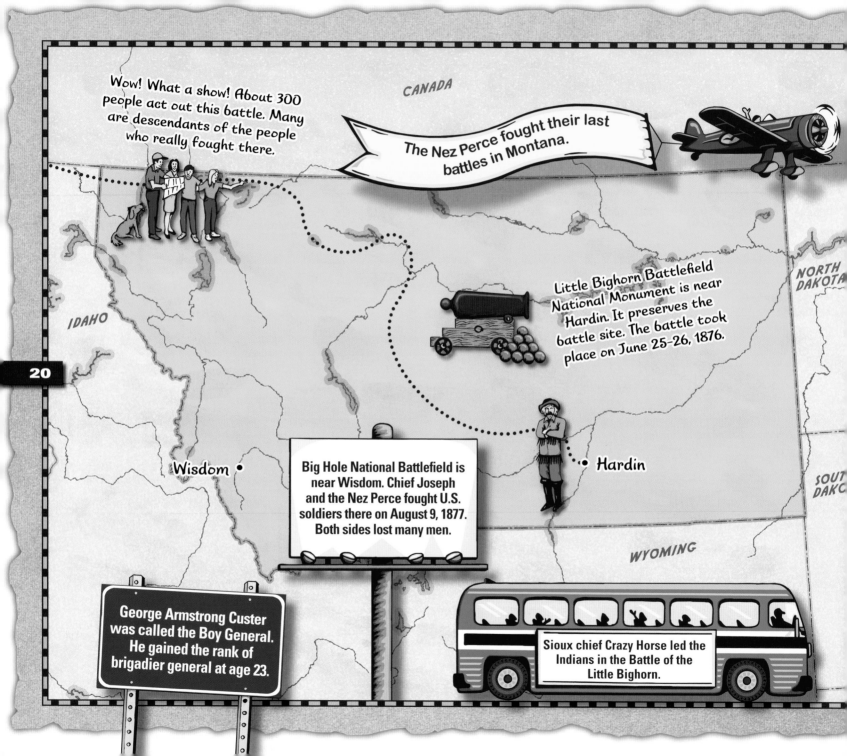

Wow! What a show! About 300 people act out this battle. Many are descendants of the people who really fought there.

CANADA

The Nez Perce fought their last battles in Montana.

Little Bighorn Battlefield National Monument is near Hardin. It preserves the battle site. The battle took place on June 25–26, 1876.

NORTH DAKOTA

IDAHO

Wisdom •

Big Hole National Battlefield is near Wisdom. Chief Joseph and the Nez Perce fought U.S. soldiers there on August 9, 1877. Both sides lost many men.

• Hardin

WYOMING

SOUTH DAKOTA

George Armstrong Custer was called the Boy General. He gained the rank of brigadier general at age 23.

Sioux chief Crazy Horse led the Indians in the Battle of the Little Bighorn.

Watching Custer's Last Stand

Indians and soldiers are locked in battle. Their cries rise amid smoke and dust. It seems like a movie. But you're right there. It's the Battle of the Little Bighorn! People act out this battle near Hardin every year.

Gold was found near this area. The U.S. government wanted the Indians out. Army officer George Custer was sent there in 1876. He was to move the Indians to reservations.

Custer attacked the Sioux and Cheyenne. But the Indians killed Custer and all his men. This battle is called Custer's Last Stand. Later, the Indians were defeated and moved.

Are you back in 1876? No, you're watching a reenactment near Hardin.

Butte's World Museum of Mining

All aboard! Get ready to tour the Orphan Girl Mine!

Montana was the 41st state to enter the Union. It joined on November 8, 1889.

Take a tour of the Orphan Girl Mine. See the mine shaft that went deep underground. People and mules traveled down in a cage. Then tour Hell Roarin' Gulch. It's built like an 1890s mining town. You can even try panning for gold. You're exploring Butte's World Museum of Mining!

Gold mining began in Butte in 1864. Then silver was discovered in 1875. Next, copper was discovered in Butte Hill. The town of Butte is on the south-facing slope of this hill. Soon it was called the Richest Hill on Earth.

The Anaconda Mining Company operated dozens of mines. **Immigrants** from many countries came to work there.

22

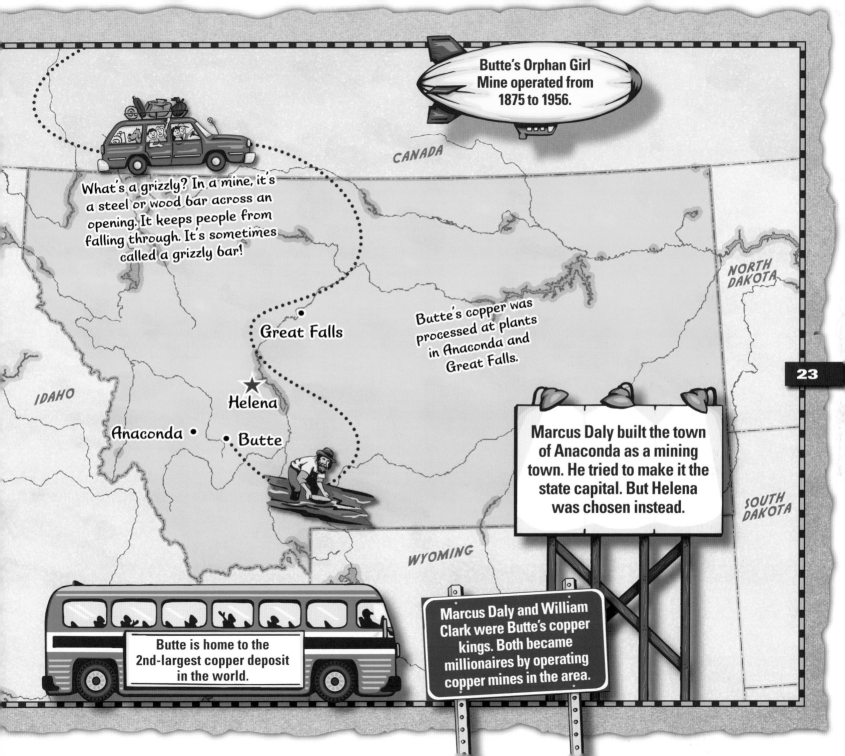

Butte's Orphan Girl Mine operated from 1875 to 1956.

What's a grizzly? In a mine, it's a steel or wood bar across an opening. It keeps people from falling through. It's sometimes called a grizzly bar!

CANADA

NORTH DAKOTA

Butte's copper was processed at plants in Anaconda and Great Falls.

Great Falls

IDAHO

★ Helena

Anaconda • • Butte

Marcus Daly built the town of Anaconda as a mining town. He tried to make it the state capital. But Helena was chosen instead.

SOUTH DAKOTA

WYOMING

Butte is home to the 2nd-largest copper deposit in the world.

Marcus Daly and William Clark were Butte's copper kings. Both became millionaires by operating copper mines in the area.

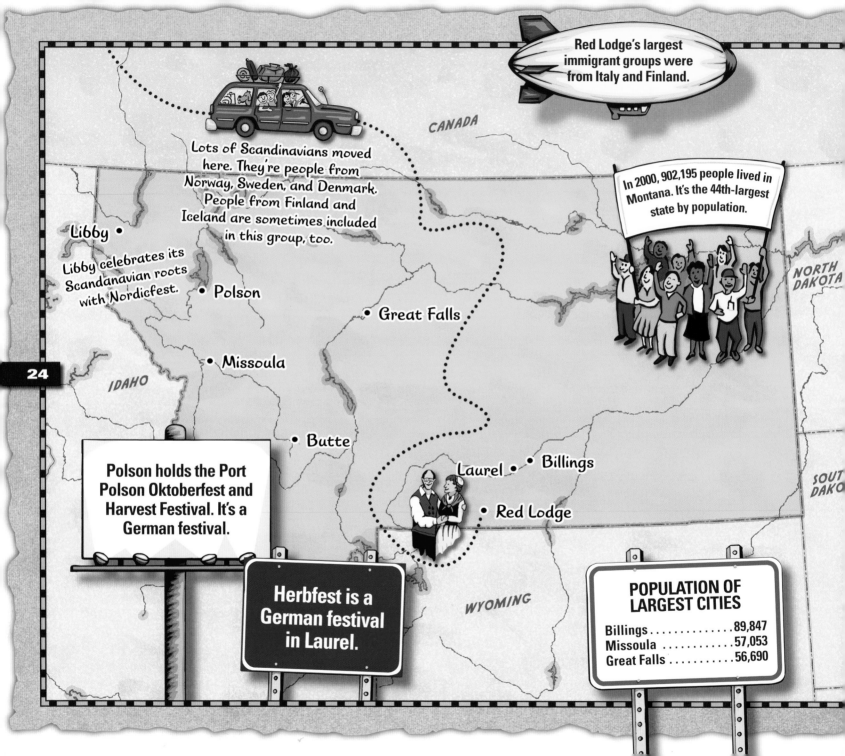

Red Lodge's largest immigrant groups were from Italy and Finland.

Lots of Scandinavians moved here. They're people from Norway, Sweden, and Denmark. People from Finland and Iceland are sometimes included in this group, too.

In 2000, 902,195 people lived in Montana. It's the 44th-largest state by population.

CANADA

Libby •

Libby celebrates its Scandanavian roots with Nordicfest.

• Polson

• Great Falls

NORTH DAKOTA

• Missoula

IDAHO

• Butte

Laurel • • Billings

SOUT DAKO

• Red Lodge

Polson holds the Port Polson Oktoberfest and Harvest Festival. It's a German festival.

Herbfest is a German festival in Laurel.

WYOMING

POPULATION OF LARGEST CITIES

Billings 89,847
Missoula 57,053
Great Falls 56,690

The Festival of Nations in Red Lodge

Want to dance? Kick up your heels at the Festival of Nations!

Dancers whirl around to lively tunes. They wear costumes from many lands. And what's that smell? It could be German, Italian, or Scottish food. You're enjoying Red Lodge's Festival of Nations!

Many immigrants settled in this coal-mining town. Some came from England, Ireland, Wales, or Scotland. Others came from Germany, Italy, Finland, or Norway. Not everyone worked in the mines. Many settlers kept farms and ranches.

Butte also welcomed many immigrants. Miners arrived from Ireland, England, and Wales. People came from eastern Europe and China, too. It's great to enjoy their customs at festivals!

Billings celebrates people from many backgrounds in its Festival of Cultures.

Visit the state capitol in Helena. There you'll see Montana lawmakers in action.

The State Capitol in Helena

See that shiny dome on top of the capitol? Guess what it's made of. Copper, of course! Copper played a big part in Montana's history. No wonder it tops the state government building.

Montana's government is divided into three branches. One branch makes the laws. Its members meet in the capitol. Another branch carries out the laws. The governor heads this branch. Judges make up the third branch. They listen to cases in courts. Then they decide whether laws have been broken.

In the capitol is a giant painting by famous Montana cowboy artist Charles M. Russell. It's called *Lewis and Clark Meeting Indians at Ross' Hole*.

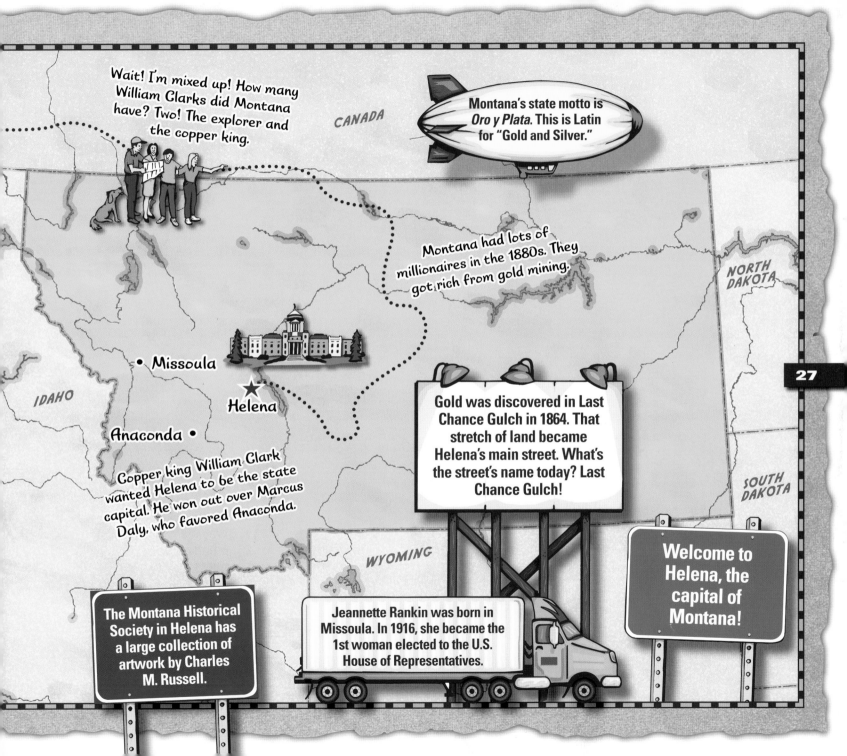

Wait! I'm mixed up! How many William Clarks did Montana have? Two! The explorer and the copper king.

CANADA

Montana's state motto is *Oro y Plata*. This is Latin for "Gold and Silver."

Montana had lots of millionaires in the 1880s. They got rich from gold mining.

NORTH DAKOTA

• Missoula

★ Helena

Anaconda •

Copper king William Clark wanted Helena to be the state capital. He won out over Marcus Daly, who favored Anaconda.

IDAHO

Gold was discovered in Last Chance Gulch in 1864. That stretch of land became Helena's main street. What's the street's name today? Last Chance Gulch!

SOUTH DAKOTA

WYOMING

The Montana Historical Society in Helena has a large collection of artwork by Charles M. Russell.

Jeannette Rankin was born in Missoula. In 1916, she became the 1st woman elected to the U.S. House of Representatives.

Welcome to Helena, the capital of Montana!

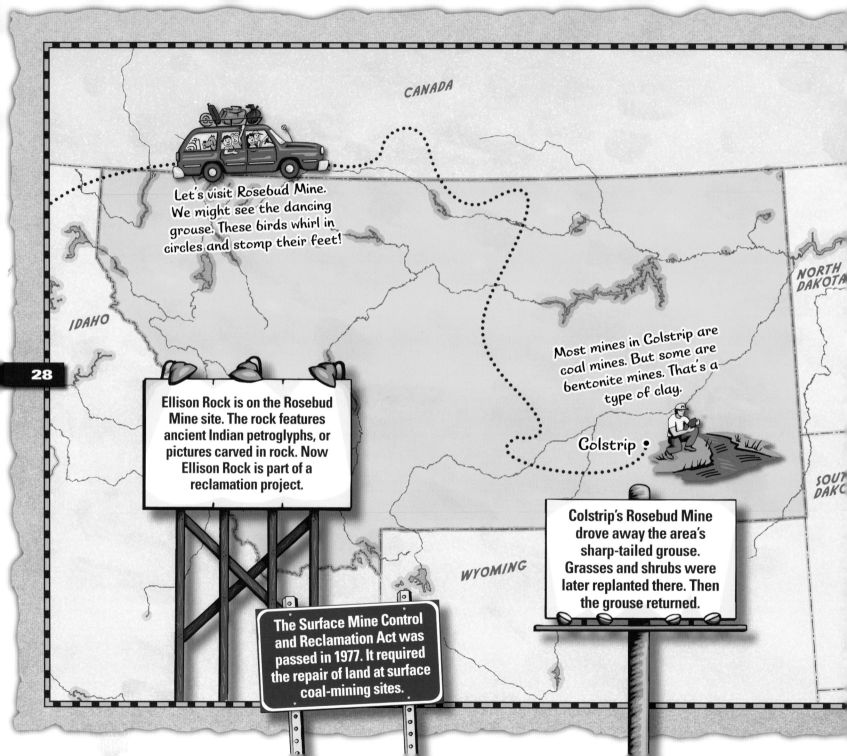

CANADA

IDAHO

NORTH DAKOTA

28

Let's visit Rosebud Mine. We might see the dancing grouse. These birds whirl in circles and stomp their feet!

Most mines in Colstrip are coal mines. But some are bentonite mines. That's a type of clay.

Ellison Rock is on the Rosebud Mine site. The rock features ancient Indian petroglyphs, or pictures carved in rock. Now Ellison Rock is part of a reclamation project.

Colstrip •

SOUTH DAKOTA

Colstrip's Rosebud Mine drove away the area's sharp-tailed grouse. Grasses and shrubs were later replanted there. Then the grouse returned.

WYOMING

The Surface Mine Control and Reclamation Act was passed in 1977. It required the repair of land at surface coal-mining sites.

Cleaning Up in Colstrip

Most mining goes on underground. But sometimes valuable minerals lie near the surface. Miners scoop out the land to get them.

Surface mining began in Colstrip in the 1920s. The pits and dirt piles became a terrible mess. In the 1970s, Colstrip began to clean up. Its mines began massive reclamation projects. Reclamation involves repairing damaged land.

You can see how these areas look now. They have grassy land and clean, sparkling streams. One area was once a home for sharp-tailed grouse. The males do a dance to attract females. Now their dancing ground is back again!

The sharp-tailed grouse calls Colstrip home.

Colstrip's Big Sky Mine has planted grasses, evened out the land, and created water channels.

Making Guitars in Bozeman

See sheets of wood stacked to the ceiling. Watch workers cut curves and circles in the wood. See other workers add pearly shell designs. What's the finished product? A beautiful guitar!

You're touring Bozeman's Gibson guitar factory. It makes one of Montana's many wood products. Other factories make lumber, pencils, and telephone poles!

Montana's major factory activity is oil refinement. That means removing impure materials from oil. Montana has lots of food-processing plants, too. They process meat, milk, and grains.

Whoa! A lot of work goes into making 1 guitar!

Eastern Montana has the country's largest supply of coal.

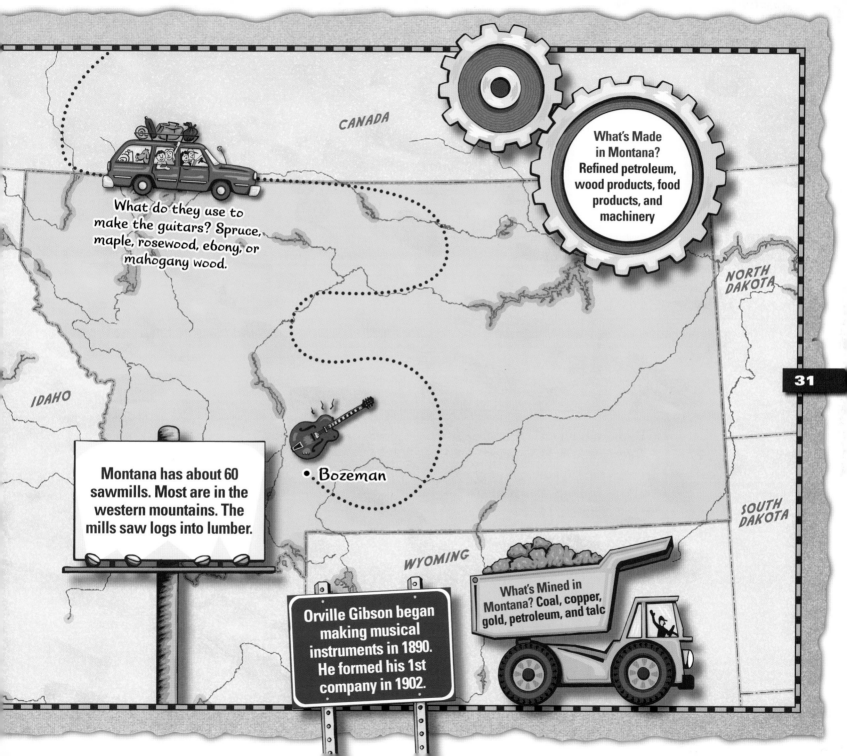

CANADA

What do they use to make the guitars? Spruce, maple, rosewood, ebony, or mahogany wood.

What's Made in Montana? Refined petroleum, wood products, food products, and machinery

NORTH DAKOTA

IDAHO

Montana has about 60 sawmills. Most are in the western mountains. The mills saw logs into lumber.

• Bozeman

SOUTH DAKOTA

WYOMING

What's Mined in Montana? Coal, copper, gold, petroleum, and talc

Orville Gibson began making musical instruments in 1890. He formed his 1st company in 1902.

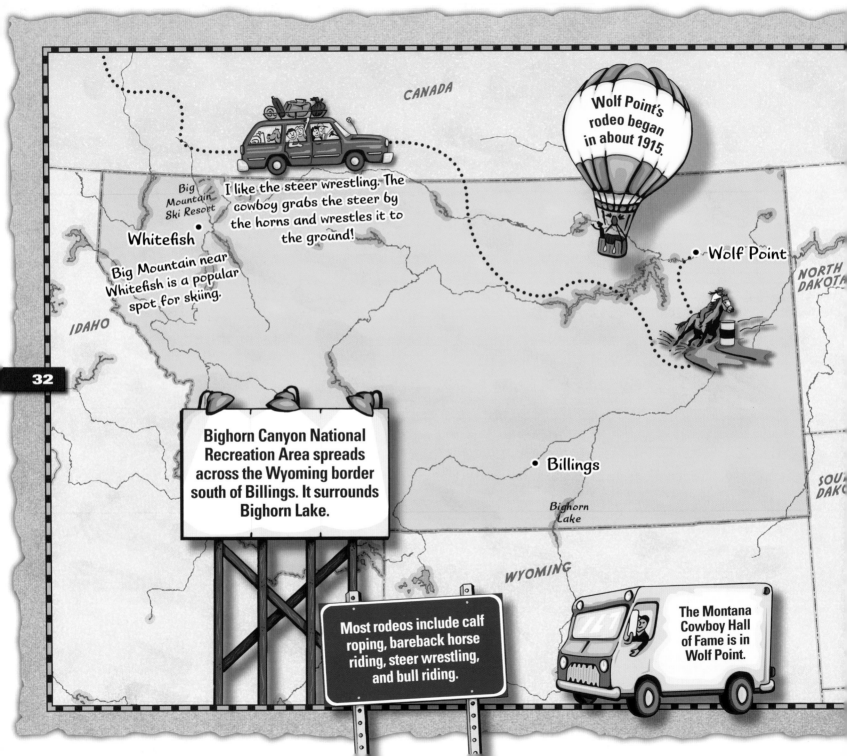

CANADA

Wolf Point's rodeo began in about 1915.

Big Mountain Ski Resort

Whitefish

I like the steer wrestling. The cowboy grabs the steer by the horns and wrestles it to the ground!

Big Mountain near Whitefish is a popular spot for skiing.

IDAHO

• Wolf Point

NORTH DAKOTA

32

Bighorn Canyon National Recreation Area spreads across the Wyoming border south of Billings. It surrounds Bighorn Lake.

• Billings

Bighorn Lake

SOUTH DAKOTA

WYOMING

Most redeos include calf roping, bareback horse riding, steer wrestling, and bull riding.

The Montana Cowboy Hall of Fame is in Wolf Point.

Wolf Point's Wild Horse Stampede

Wild horses run madly around the ring. Three cowboys chase them on foot. They hope to catch a horse and saddle it. Then they'll try to ride it. You're watching the Wild Horse Stampede!

This is Montana's oldest rodeo. It features many other riding and roping events. Almost every Montana town holds a rodeo. Cowboys and cowgirls show off their skills there.

Montana's a great place for outdoor adventures, too. People love camping, hiking, and mountain climbing. Boaters and fishers enjoy the lakes and streams. In the winter, people go snowmobiling and skiing. And everyone likes to gaze at the Big Sky!

Ride 'em, cowgirl! Be sure to catch a Montana rodeo.

In the 1800s, people in Wolf Point worked at trapping wolves and trading their hides.

Smoke jumpers can't be afraid of heights. This trainee takes to the skies over Missoula.

The Missoula smoke jumpers fight fires all over the western United States.

Smoke Jumping in Missoula

Would you like to be a firefighter? Would you like to fight forest fires? How about parachuting out of an airplane? Some people do all these things at once. They're called smoke jumpers!

Just drop by Missoula's Smokejumper Visitor Center. You'll learn how smoke jumpers train and work. You'll see the **loft** where they practice jumps.

More than eighty men and women work here. When a fire call comes, the action begins. They suit up and board an aircraft. They parachute into burning wilderness areas. Whatever it takes, they bravely battle raging fires. Would you like to be a smoke jumper?

34

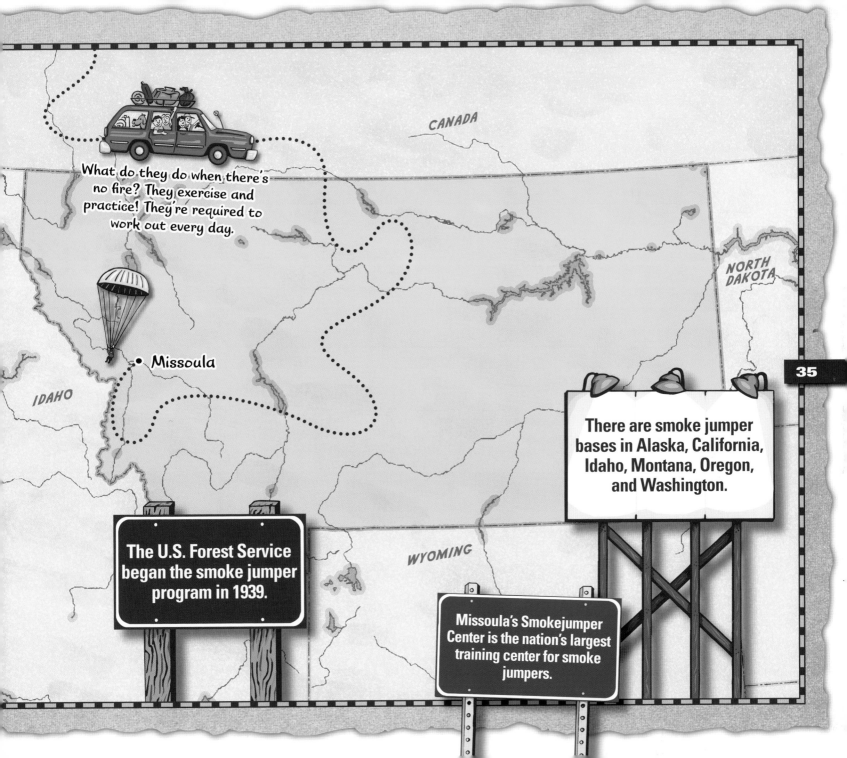

What do they do when there's no fire? They exercise and practice! They're required to work out every day.

CANADA

NORTH DAKOTA

IDAHO

• Missoula

There are smoke jumper bases in Alaska, California, Idaho, Montana, Oregon, and Washington.

WYOMING

The U.S. Forest Service began the smoke jumper program in 1939.

Missoula's Smokejumper Center is the nation's largest training center for smoke jumpers.

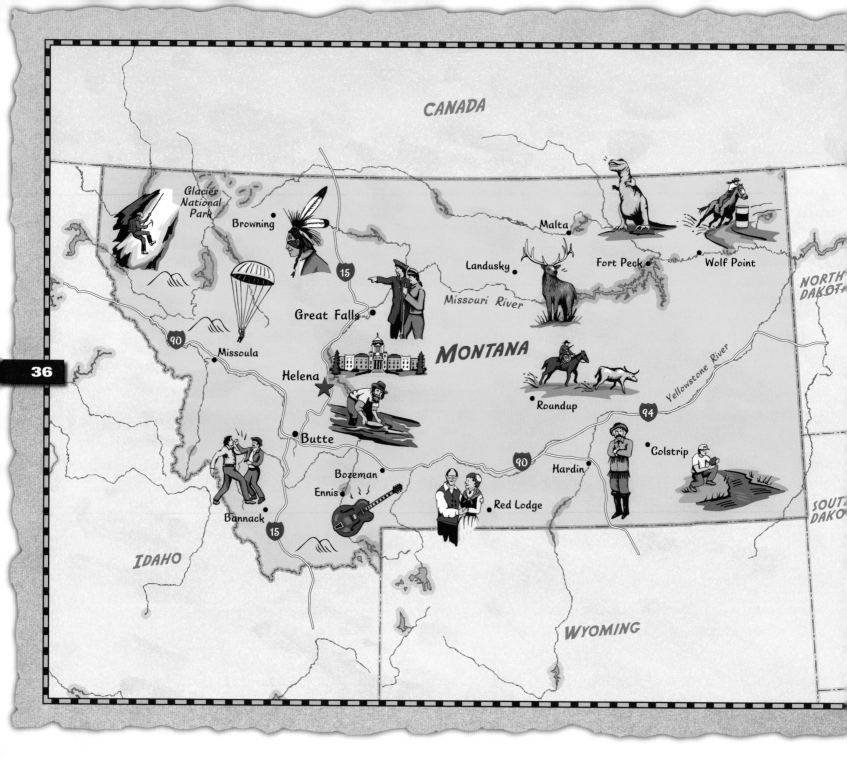

OUR TRIP

We visited many amazing places on our trip! We also met a lot of interesting people along the way. Look at the map on the left. Use your finger to trace all the places we have been.

What is the biggest waterfall on the Missouri River? See page 7 for the answer.

How many dinosaur museums and dig sites are on the Montana Dinosaur Trail? Page 10 has the answer.

What does *Maiasaura* mean? Look on page 11 for the answer.

What is Montana's largest Indian group? Page 13 has the answer.

When did Lewis and Clark camp at Great Falls? Page 15 has the answer.

What was the name of Montana's 1st capital? Turn to page 16 for the answer.

Who was the 1st woman elected to the U.S. House of Representatives? Look on page 27 for the answer.

Where is the Montana Cowboy Hall of Fame located? Turn to page 32 for the answer.

That was a great trip! We have traveled all over Montana.

There are a few places that we didn't have time for, though. Next time, we plan to go on a Spirit of the North Sled Dog Adventure in Ennis. A team of huskies pulls visitors over a mountain trail. The huskies are very friendly and love being out in the snow!

More Places to Visit in Montana

WORDS TO KNOW

descendants (di-SEND-uhnts) someone's children, grandchildren, great-grandchildren, and so on

fossil (FOSS-uhl) a remain or print of an animal or plant that lived long ago

hosts (HOHSTS) people who open their homes or territory to guests

immigrants (IM-uh-gruhnts) people who leave their home country and move to another country

loft (LOFT) a platform high above the ground floor

reservation (rez-ur-VAY-shuhn) land set aside for a special purpose, such as for Native Americans

vigilante (vig-uh-LAN-tee) member of a group of people who fight crime and carry out justice themselves

wilderness (WIL-dur-niss) a natural area that's rough and wild

Montana covers 145,552 square miles (376,979 sq km). It's the 4th-largest state in size.

STATE SYMBOLS

State animal: Grizzly bear

State bird: Western meadowlark

State butterfly: Mourning cloak

State fish: Blackspotted cutthroat trout

State flower: Bitterroot

State fossil: *Maiasaura* (duck-billed dinosaur)

State gemstones: Agate and sapphire

State grass: Bluebunch wheatgrass

State tree: Ponderosa pine

State flag

State seal

STATE SONGS

"Montana"

Words by Charles C. Cohan, music by Joseph E. Howard

Tell me of that Treasure State
Story always new,
Tell of its beauties grand
And its hearts so true.
Mountains of sunset fire
The land I love the best
Let me grasp the hand of one
From out the golden West.

Chorus:
Montana, Montana,
Glory of the West
Of all the states from coast to coast,
You're easily the best.
Montana, Montana,
Where skies are always blue
M-O-N-T-A-N-A,
Montana, I love you.

Each country has its flow'r;
Each one plays a part,
Each bloom brings a longing hope
To some lonely heart.
Bitterroot to me is dear
Growing in my land
Sing then that glorious air
The one I understand.

(Chorus)

FAMOUS PEOPLE

Bergoust, Eric (1969–), skier and Olympic gold medalist

Carvey, Dana (1955–), comedian

Cooper, Gary (1901–1961), actor

Horner, Jack (1946–), paleontologist

Huntley, Chet (1911–1974), television newscaster

Jackson, Phil (1945–), basketball coach

Knievel, Evel (1938–), daredevil

Kramer, Jerry (1936–), football player

Loy, Myrna (1905–1993), actor

Lynch, David (1946–), screenwriter and director

Maclean, Norman (1902–1990), author and teacher

Mansfield, Mike (1903–2001), politician

McNally, Dave (1942–2002), baseball player

Montgomery, George (1916–2000), actor

Patent, Dorothy Hinshaw (1940–), children's author

Plenty Coups (ca. 1848–1932), American Indian leader

Rankin, Jeannette (1880–1973), politician

Russell, Charles Marion (1864–1926), painter

Swingley, Doug (1953–), Iditarod sled dog race champion

Washakie (ca. 1804–1900), American Indian leader

TO FIND OUT MORE

At the Library
Collard, Sneed B. *B Is for Big Sky Country: A Montana Alphabet.* Chelsea, Mich.: Sleeping Bear Press, 2003.

Gray, Susan Heinrichs. *Maiasaura.* Chanhassen, Minn.: The Child's World, 2004.

Kavasch, E. Barrie. *Crow Children and Elders Talk Together.* New York: PowerKids Press, 1999.

Peterson, Cris, and Alvis Upitis (photographer). *Amazing Grazing.* Honesdale, Pa.: Boyds Mill Press, 2002.

Trumbauer, Lisa. *Montana.* New York: Children's Press, 2003.

On the Web
Visit our home page for lots of links about Montana: *http://www.childsworld.com/links*

Note to Parents, Teachers, and Librarians: We routinely verify our Web links to make sure they are safe, active sites—so encourage your readers to check them out!

Places to Visit or Contact
Montana Historical Society
PO Box 201201
225 North Roberts
Helena, MT 59629
406/444-2694
For more information about the history of Montana

Travel Montana
301 South Park
PO Box 200533
Helena, MT 59620
800/847-4868
For more information about traveling in Montana

INDEX

Bye, Big Sky Country. We had a great time. We'll come back soon!